G000093113

THE QUALITY OF MERCY

Concerning the life and crimes of
Dr. Harold Frederick Shipman

by Edwin Flay

Published by Playdead Press 2022

© Edwin Flay 2022

Edwin Flay has asserted his rights under the Copyright, Design and Patents Act, 1988, to be identified as the author of this work.

A CIP catalogue record for this book is available from the British Library.

ISBN 978-1-915533-04-3

Caution

All rights whatsoever in this play are strictly reserved and application for performance should be sought through the author before rehearsals begin. No performance may be given unless a license has been obtained.

This book is sold subject to the condition that it shall not by way of trade or otherwise, be lent, resold, hired out, or otherwise circulated without the publisher's prior consent in any form of binding or cover other than that in which it is published and without a similar condition including this condition being imposed on the subsequent purchaser.

Playdead Press
www.playdeadpress.com

CAST AND CREATIVES

CAST
Fred | **Edwin Flay**

Detective | **Christian Ballantyne**

Solicitor | **Chris Rogers**

Newsreader | **John Waite**

CREATIVES
Writer and performer | **Edwin Flay**

Director and Dramaturg | **Bernie C. Byrnes**

Producer | **Sarah Lawrie**

Sound Designer | **Kirsty Gillmore**

Lighting Designer & Production Manager | **Adam Bottomley**

Videographer | **Neil Monaghan**

Stage Manager | **Becky Brown**

Associate Producer | **Kat Rogers**

Press Officer | **Matthew Parker**

EDWIN FLAY
Writer & Performer

Edwin Flay studied Film & Drama at The University of Reading, graduating in 1998, and now works as an actor, writer and producer. Television credits include OUTLANDER (Amazon Prime), THE SUFFRAGETTES (BBC), BOOMERS (BBC) and TO WAR! (BBC). Film credits include THE CARROT (Another Footnote Ltd), SERVANTS' QUARTERS (Aviary Films), CROWHURST (Splash Page Media), REFUGEE (CTVC) and GRACE OF MONACO (Stone Angels). Theatre credits include RICHARD II (The Vaults), MOONLIGHT & MAGNOLIAS (English Theatre of Hamburg), A LA CARTE (Southwark Playhouse), THE TAILOR-MADE MAN (The White Bear), THE CRYSTAL EGG (The Vaults), THE BRIGHTON KILLERS (Brighton Fringe), and THE HOUSE (So & So Arts Club). In 2021, he made his Radio 4 debut in the legal drama BARRED (B7 Media).

Edwin wrote, produced and appeared in a short film called AN UNKIND WORD, which played to festivals worldwide, winning an Indie Spirit Award at Idyllwild and a Bronze Remi at Worldfest Houston. He has also written multiple feature screenplays. THE QUALITY OF MERCY is Edwin's first stage play. Twitter: @EdwinFlay

BERNIE C. BYRNES
Director & Dramaturg

Bernie C. Byrnes is a multi-award-winning writer and director, and holds a PhD in Literary Criticism. Bernie was Dramaturg on award winning shows MUSE OF FIRE (Shakespeare's Globe) and LITTLE SOLDIERS (Theatre Re).

International work includes projects in Poland, Switzerland, the USA, Mumbai and Singapore. Previous commissions include the RSC, Soho Theatre, Channel 5, Pluto Productions, Digital Catapult and Blackwatch Entertainment.

Bernie is an established theatrical practitioner, a Fellow of the Royal Society of Arts and a member of the Guild of Directors. She has worked alongside Stephen Pimlott, Ed Hall, Michael Attenborough, Gareth Armstrong and Wayne Sleep. Bernie's specialist interests are Mental Health, Art & Vulnerable Communities, and New Writing.

Twitter: @BernieCByrnes

SARAH LAWRIE
Producer

Sarah Lawrie has been making theatre since 2013. Most recently she produced Arts Council funded web series LEAR ALONE, which won Best Series at Off West End's OnComm Awards 2022. Other recent work includes ASSISTED (The Space @EdFringe – nominated for The Popcorn Award for New Writing in partnership with BBC Writers' Room), LOVE & DESTRUCTION (Playground Theatre), LEAVES (Jermyn Street Theatre), SCROUNGER (Finborough Theatre – winner of Best New Play at the Off West End Awards 2021), web series LATE NIGHT STARING AT HIGH RES PIXELS (winner of London Pub Theatre's Standing Ovation Award for Best Theatre Online) and TIMELESS (Space Theatre and touring). Sarah is a founding member of And Tomorrow Theatre Company, whose inaugural production DEATH OF A HUNTER premiered at the Finborough Theatre in 2018 and transferred to the Brighton Fringe Festival.

Sarah is also the co-creator and sole producer of Rula Lenska's one woman show FROM DZIKOW TO WILLESDEN GREEN and is currently developing SHUTTERS: A LESBIAN ROCK OPERA for The Vindicate Company.

Twitter: @La_Lawrie

KIRSTY GILLMORE
Sound Designer

Kirsty Gillmore is an award-winning sound designer, director and the owner of Sounds Wilde. She has worked in professional sound for over twenty years, sound designing, recording and mixing for theatre, opera and audio and radio drama.

Theatre and opera credits include THE GRAVITY (Bristol Old Vic), KILL CLIMATE DENIERS (Pleasance), THE SHAPE OF THE PAIN (Battersea Arts Centre), L'OSPEDALE (Wilton's) and THE LITTLE PRINCE (Arcola).

Audio and radio drama credits include PERSUASION (Audible), THE SPACE RACE (Audible/B7 Media), GREENBORNE (B7 Media) and THE SANDMAN: ACT II (Audible Original), based on the cult graphic novels by Neil Gaiman.

Kirsty is also an acclaimed voice director and casting director for games and animation. Recent titles include LIVEALIVE (Square Enix), DESTRUCTION ALLSTARS (Lucid Games) and BALDUR'S GATE 3 (Larian Studios.) In 2021 she was chosen for the prestigious BAFTA Breakthrough UK programme as a Voice Director for Games.

Twitter: @SoundsWilde

ADAM BOTTOMLEY

Lighting Designer & Production Manager

Adam Bottomley is a freelance Set Builder, Lighting Designer and Production Manager with a diverse portfolio ranging from Touring Opera and Musical Theatre to Festivals, Fringe theatre and site-specific productions. Lighting Design credits include POLICE COPS THE MUSICAL (New Diorama) and BADASS BE THY NAME (international tour), HUSH NOW (Courtyard Theatre, Hereford), THE SPIRAL PATH (White Bear Theatre and Maltings Arts Theatre, St Albans) and JOURNEY'S END at the Kruitmagazijn, Ypres.

Twitter: @AdamBottomley

NEIL MONAGHAN

Videographer

Neil Monaghan is a writer and director for film, theatre, television and radio. He trained with the BBC, working in post-production for the Film Department, and subsequently left to set up his own production company. He has written several award-winning shorts, as well as multiple feature films.

His first feature, MADE IN ROMANIA, a comedy 'mockumentary' about independent filmmaking, starred Jason Flemyng, Jennifer Tilly and Elizabeth Hurley. His debut feature as a writer & director, ELECTION NIGHT, a home-invasion movie that examines societal division and the rise of right-wing populism, has won numerous awards, including best feature and best screenplay at film festivals worldwide.

Twitter: @NMonaghanFilm

BECKY BROWN
Stage Manager

Becky Brown graduated with BA (Hons) Theatre Production from Bath Spa University in 2014. Credits include: LITTLE MANFRED, ARMY GIRL & SOLDIER ON (The Soldiers Arts Academy); THE SECRET DIARY OF ADRIAN MOLE THE MUSICAL (Queens Theatre Hornchurch); THE SPIRAL PATH (KatAlyst); LA NONNE SANGLANTE (Gothic Opera); THE GOAL, JACK & THE BEANSTALK, PETER PAN and SLEEPING BEAUTY (Courtyard Theatre, Hereford); THE COMEDY OF ERRORS, HENRY V, PETER PAN (OVO); HUSH NOW (Feral Productions); MEDICINE'S MONSTROUS DAUGHTERS (Vital Xposure); RELATIVELY SPEAKING, CALIFORNIA SUITE (Carnival UK); THE BEST OF... ROCK MUSICALS (Eventim Apollo); CRY HAVOC (Park Theatre); THE TEMPEST (Southwark Playhouse).

Twitter: @Becky_Brown14

Nailed Productions

Nailed Productions is a production company working in the creative arts run by Edwin Flay in collaboration with Neil Monaghan, which started life as Nailed Films.

After the completion and successful festival run of their first short film, *AN UNKIND WORD,* starring Robert Daws and Susan Penhaligon, they moved into theatre production: *THE QUALITY OF MERCY* is their first play.

Writer's Note

When I started writing this play, I had a somewhat different perspective on Harold Shipman. My mother Eileen and I had visited my grandmother Renee Lacey two weeks before he killed her: most of the time, she was lost in the depths of advanced dementia, veering between fear and belligerence as she tried to make sense of the strange faces that surrounded her. In the few hours that Renee was coherent, she was desperately unhappy and ashamed, a headstrong, fiercely house-proud woman appalled at the grimy windows and the dusty carpets that she was in no condition to clean.

So when it emerged that Shipman had unlawfully taken Renee's life, Eileen and I were quite equivocal about it. Obviously, no person should ever euthanise another without their consent, but having seen the state she was in, the act seemed to me to come from a place of kindness, however misplaced (this was not a view shared by my aunt Anne, who never liked Shipman, never trusted him, and suspected his involvement in Renee's death immediately). My own abiding memory of the man who was my first GP was inevitably quite foggy – a kindly fellow with a big bushy beard who had a bowl of midget gems on his desk for a brave child that didn't make a fuss during check-ups.

It was these two first impressions that led me to start researching his history, with a view to painting a more nuanced picture of Shipman than the tabloids had ever bothered to do. Three weeks later, I threw away my notes, having concluded that he was irredeemable, a narcissistic psychopath every bit as bad as the papers had made him out to be.

The thing that drew me back was ultimately discovering that other people seemed to have drawn the same initial, erroneous conclusion as I had: I remember mentioning him to someone, who replied "Oh yeah, he helped a few old dears over the threshold." Society, it seemed, was forgetting the sheer scale of his crimes, and had never grasped the depths of cruelty to which he would descend in order to satisfy his need to kill. I was compelled to give the audience a similar revelation to the one that I had experienced.

Due to his silence right up to the moment of his suicide, Shipman remains a profoundly unknowable figure. In researching and developing this piece, I leaned very heavily on the evidence from the psychological analyses conducted for the Smith Report into Shipman's career. The entire report is publicly available through the National Archives website; it would not have been possible to write this play without it.

There is a growing – and welcome – trend in media about serial killers to focus on the victims, rather than the killers, which a one-man show about Shipman cannot hope to reflect. However, I have tried, through the use of back projection, to keep the victims always in the mind of the audience, and to drive home the extent and senselessness of his crimes.

I would like to thank Andrew Piper, Jerome Wright, Cate Fowler, Camille Wilhelm, Sarah Berger, Neil Monaghan and Bernie C Byrnes for helping me in developing the script; Siva Zagel and everyone at the Courtyard Theatre for their support in staging the play; my late mother Eileen and my aunt Anne for giving their approval to the project; and most importantly Kirsty, who has supported me every step of the way, putting up with me at my worst and always making me sound my best.

Edwin Flay

For Renee,
and for all of the victims.

For Jim, and Eileen, and Anne,
and for all of the relatives.

ACT I

Scene 1

A prison cell is the set for the entire play, the different scenes signified by lighting and sound changes, and sometimes a quick move of the furniture in the action.

Footage of an interview with Shipman from 2002 is projected onto the back wall. A DETECTIVE holds a folder of photographs and periodically holds one up for Fred to look at.

DETECTIVE: I have here a photograph of Lily Crossley, if you'd like to look at that.

Beat.

> Just for the benefit of the tape, Dr Shipman's eyes are closed and he didn't look at the photograph at all.

He swaps it for another photograph.

> That's Elizabeth Pearce. Out of the three ladies there, it's the elderly lady dressed in black.

Beat.

> For the record, Dr Shipman's eyes are closed, and he did not look at the photograph.

The footage ends, and the stage is dark.

Scene 2

The prison cell. Wide awake and fully dressed, FRED sits on a single bed stage left. A barred window is mounted high up on the wall centre stage. A basic chair sits next to a small table stage right, which houses a battered old battery-powered radio cassette player, alongside a few cassette tapes, a jar of instant coffee, and a half-eaten packet of biscuits. Moonlight shines through the barred window.

The bed appears to be made, the sheets turned down. The "turn-down" is actually made of three lengths of torn bedsheet, neatly stacked on one another. This will become relevant.

The performance space is defined by the outer edges of the bed on stage left and the table stage right - these mark the walls of the cell. Fred only ever moves within these tiny, cramped parameters.

Standing quietly, Fred puts his slippers on, moves to the table and puts on his glasses. He picks up a cassette, slots it into the cassette player and presses "record". He waits five seconds.

FRED: Testing, testing.

He rewinds it, plays it back. "Testing, testing" can be heard coming from the speakers. He rewinds it again, presses record, waits five seconds.

I've been thinking a lot lately about the record. About what the world will think of me after I'm gone. A man starts approaching the end of his life, he can't help but dwell a bit on his legacy. Especially one as misunderstood as my own. Apparently, Brady's been saying I'm "boring." You can't help thinking that when a psychopath convicted of raping and murdering five children is passing judgement on you, then maybe it's time to present your own version of events. I maintain it was the right choice not to give evidence to that inquiry, I wasn't about to be a willing participant in my own crucifixion, but... I started to thinking about how, if I didn't put my own side of it down, then that bloody Report and the smears of the gutter press would be all that's left of me. I can't have that.

I could never bear to see anything suffer. *(beat)* Physical pain, it's a warning. It's there to tell you something is wrong. But once you know it, once you spot it, the pain itself is needless. Inflicting pain, that's the greatest cruelty I can imagine. Taking it away... well, there's nothing nobler, wouldn't you say? I used to say "I don't believe in keeping them going," because how could you, in good conscience, when you saw people in pain every day, like I did?

I remember when me mum died. I was 16 when it got to her, or at least when we knew it was in her. Cancer, of course. When you're a doctor, and I'm a very good doctor, I've passed all my exams, you're supposed to be clinical about disease. See it for what it is, cure it or cut it out as need be. But there's something wicked about cancer. The way it forms. The way it spreads. The way it can sit, undetected, for years, and then kill the patient within weeks of being discovered.

It's a cruel sickness. A group of cells goes rogue in an organ in the body, and begin growing beyond their normal limits, they become a thing of their own, a tumour. They begin to seed cells into other organs, and before you know it, the body is riddled with secondary cancers. I had a patient once, thirty fags a day for forty years. He'd done six months of radium chemotherapy, and I had to give him good news and bad news. I said to him, the good news is that you no longer have cancer in your brain, your liver, your spine or your pancreas – that's how far it can spread. He got brain cancer from smoking! – I didn't know I had pancreatic cancer, he said. Well you did, I said, but you don't. He said, what's the bad news, then? I said, your lungs are still riddled with it, and they will do for you in the end. Poor sod.

And that's what did for my mum in the end. She was such a strong woman, it was awful to see what she was reduced to. A crumpled husk. Thoughts difficult. Speaking difficult. So much pain, she could barely sit up and look out the window by the end. Hard to think of her, imperious and houseproud as she was, stuck in that room all day. Dad was working, Pauline was married and out the house by then, and Clive was only 12. They'd scrimped and saved to send me to the local grammar, I had to do as well as I could at school for her sake, and I'd have to try and keep the house going when I got home. But my first duty, soon as I got back from school every day, was always to her.

Scene 3

Through a lighting change, the cell becomes Vera Shipman's bedroom. Warm light on the bed, the sounds of a suburban northern town in the early 60s bleed in. Fred steps into the light timidly. A radio plays a snippet from the BBC Light Programme in the background.

FRED: (*softly*) Mum? Mum, it's me, I'm home.

How are you feeling today, Mum? You're looking a bit peaky.

Right. Well, same's better than worse, in't it? I got the results back on my biology test today. Got 84% - top of the class!

Well no, Mum, it's not perfect, no. But I went over the answers and worked out where I went wrong, I'll do better next time.

Don't worry, I'll go and pick Clive up when the doctor's been. I want to – Oh Mum! What is it, where's it hurt? Can I get you owt? A cup of tea? Glass of water?

Long pause. He looks at his watch.

It's 4.30. He should be here in the next half-hour or so. We got out of games a bit late, and the bus had already gone, I had to wait for the next one. I came straight home, I didn't go into town with Alan and that lot.

No, Mum.

No, Mum. I didn't, I went to the libra—

No, Mum.

I know. I do. I know how hard Dad works.

Sorry. Shall I get you that cup of tea? Pick you up a bit, a nice cup of tea.

Scene 4

The prison cell.

FRED: Forty-three. Forty-three years old, and being eaten alive by some malignant tumour. You can't tell me that's right, you can't. I don't care if you're an atheist, or you believe in a merciful God, or even a vengeful one: if there's a physical manifestation of evil in this world, it's cancer.

My mother had two things to look forward to on any given day. One was when I'd come home, and I'd try to take her mind off the pain by telling her about my day. What lessons I had. What the other kids got up to. If I'd scored a try during games. Sometimes, she'd see me. Say my name, Fred – I've always gone by Fred, to avoid confusion with me dad, who was also Harold. More often, though, she'd stare at the ceiling, her breathing ragged, and she'd clench my hand tight. Not because I'd said owt important; because she could feel the cancer growing inside her. The other thing she looked forward to was the doctor, and the injections he'd give her.

I hated seeing her like that. Hated the weight of it on me, knowing that there was nothing I could do to make it easier for her. I never felt so powerless as when I watched her dying by degrees, and I wanted, more than anything, to be able to stop it. That's why the doctor's visits were such a relief – he could stop it, briefly, and it got me wondering whether you could stop it more permanently. He was there at the end, with me and me Dad, and Clive, and Pauline. It wasn't easy. I was watching me mum die, for God's sake, but if he couldn't ease our pain at seeing her go, he eased hers at the passing, and for that I was always grateful.

Doctors were revered when I was a lad. There was an aura about them, that they had the knowing of things that eluded most people. You could tell they were exceptional; that was why it was a natural choice for me. My A levels were already pointing me in that direction anyway, and I knew it would have made my mum proud to see me become a doctor. I was offered a place at Leeds University to study medicine, and I was there for five years. Met Primrose; got married, and had our first, Sarah Rosemary. I'd got Prim in trouble, truth be told, we hadn't planned for little Sarah. I was a bright boy, I should have known better. Still, Prim's stood by me through thick and thin. Put up with more than most wives would, especially over the last few years, so it was probably for the best.

Anyroad, I left Leeds in 1970, and went to work at Pontefract General Infirmary as a junior houseman. I never intended to work at a hospital full-time; I wanted to be a GP, working in the community. But when you've just qualified, the GMC only gives you a provisional registration, you've got to do a year at hospital to get your full registration. It was a good move though, the hospital provided us with a little house within the grounds. It was where Prim had our second, Christopher; it was where my career began in earnest.

The work was gruelling. We'd be on call every other night and every other weekend. Illness doesn't just strike during working hours, and death doesn't care what time it is when he comes calling. I loved my job, though, and I was bloody good at it – I'd passed all my exams, I could tell what was wrong with someone at a glance. More than I can say for some of my fellow housemen. They lacked confidence, they couldn't understand that you had to have conviction in your diagnoses.

I wasn't a difficult man, I don't think. I may not have been the most affable doctor on the wards, but I was hungry to learn, to show what I could do. I'll allow as I could be short with folk, but I couldn't abide indecision or hesitation, and by God I resented idiots who'd second-guess me. Registrars, senior housemen, nurses, even bloody patients! You had to know what you were doing, and you had to believe in it! It was a hospital, it was full of sick people, you couldn't stand around waiting for a registrar to come and pat you on the head and tell you that yes, the poor love with the drooping face and the slurring was having a stroke! You had to act! I couldn't be having with all these hand-wringers! I had a patient. He was not a nice man...!

Fred catches himself, takes a breath. Starts this anecdote again.

I had a patient. He was not a nice man, as it goes, but any doctor will tell you, no-one's at their best when they're in constant torment. He had emphysema and chronic bronchitis, so he didn't have long to go, and every moment was a waking hell for him.

The medical ward at Pontefract General Infirmary. The lighting is fairly dim, as befits a ward in late evening. Beeps of monitors and general sounds of malaise in the background. Footsteps squeak along shiny floors from time to time. Fred enters, checks a chart at the end of the bed, and goes to stand by it.

FRED: Hello Thomas, how are we feeling this evening?

There's no need to take that tone with me, Mr Cullumbine, I'm here for your benefit.

I'm a senior houseman on the ward, Mr Cullumbine. I've seen you before, if you don't remember me, then I'd put that down to the pain relief you're on.

Now, I hope we're not going to have any more trouble with that. We've been through all this, you can't go home, you know that.

I get that you don't want to be here. I do understand.

Mr Cullumbine. Wouldn't you rather be comfortable, tended to by professionals who've got your best interests at heart?

Very well, then. If you're so determined to go home, up you get. There's the door.

Pause.

All right, all right. I'm sorry about that.

Look, I know. I know it's wretched being stuck in bed all day in this place. But you're too sick to go anywhere on your own, and your family can't look after you in your condition. I'm sorry.

It's not for two hours, Mr Cullumbine. Ten o'clock, last rounds of the night.

Well, no. We have to stick to the schedules. Otherwise, you'll be in agony for hours after this lot wears off, the next lot won't be due till morning and there'll be no-one around to help.

Courage doesn't come into it, it's my duty.

I know you don't want to be here –

There is no call to be rude, Mr Cullumbine!

Pause.

All right, Thomas. If you want my help. I'll help you.

26

Scene 6

The prison cell.

The name "Thomas Cullumbine" appears in bright white letters against the wall of the cell. As the play continues, the names of each of Shipman's victims should be added at different places around the wall (a full list in chronological order may be found at the end of the play).

The rate of their additions increases to reflect the rate of his killings at each stage of his narrative – infrequent in the early years, thick and fast in the final stages.

They should fade out at the beginning of each flashback, and return for each scene in the cell.

FRED: He went peacefully. Do you have any idea what chronic bronchitis is like? It's like suffocating on the fluid in your lungs. You cough, and you cough, and you can't shift it. It sits there on your chest, always threatening to drown you, never finishing the job. Months, he'd endured that. Night and day. I went to bed that night, and I slept like a baby. I had grasped the nettle, stared someone's agony in its wretched face, and said enough is enough. I'd done for Thomas what I couldn't do for my mum. I had gained the power of life and death. I was 26 years old.

   I remember in court, they kept accusing me of murder; I stuck to the simple, immutable truth: "I treated them appropriately for their medical condition at the time." To this day, I maintain that there is no word of a lie in that statement.

I experimented a few more times at Pontefract. I had good results with potassium chloride, which was readily available around the wards; digoxin, aminophilline, chlorpromazine, pethidine. It was easy enough; it was a busy hospital, there was always someone close to death, who could benefit from my special attentions. I was doing what I had been put on this earth to do. I knew then what I'd always known inside, what me mum had always told me, it was all true – I had a gift.

You see, what people don't understand is that when you're faced with someone who's dying, who's actually dying right in front of you, it's a kindness to give them certainty. To help them drift away on golden waves, instead of... I've seen patients, past verbal, past any sort of movement beyond a weak nod of the head, suddenly strain their entire bodies up to heaven, eyes wide and pleading, in an attempt to escape the wasted, broken vessel that's holding them back, only to slump back down again because they don't know how to let go. But some folk, some religious folk in particular, they think easing someone's distress is a sin! Saying it should be up to God when you go, it's mediaeval. But they call it morality.

And to find a God-botherer in a hospital, well! Long story short, I had a scare. I gave someone an injection, and she passed away. So far, so normal, but a nurse put two and two together, and it turned out she'd been sniffing around some of the other deaths on the ward as well.

The nurse's station at Pontefract General Infirmary. Bright light, hospital sounds in the background. Fred walks past the table to address someone downstage.

FRED: You wanted to see me, Sister?

Not at all, what can I do for you?

Mrs Thwaites, yes. Very sad, yes. But inevitable, come the end, I think you'll agree.

As it happens, yes. There were no nurses to hand at the time, so I undertook to give her the appropriate medication myself.

Prematurely?

We can none of us choose our time, Sister, nor the manner of our passing.

I gave Mrs Thwaites 40mg of frusemide for her ventricular failure, and 0.25mg digoxin for the triple rhythm in her heart. Do you not consider that the correct dosage?

Poor timing, I suppose. It's most unfortunate, I agree.

What other patients? What injection packs?

I've no idea how they could have got there. You said it yourself, I diagnose and prescribe. It's the nursing staff who administer the drugs. What exactly are you getting at?

Just to be absolutely clear, Sister, are you suggesting Mrs Thwaites died by accident, or by design?

I'm just trying to see where you're going with all this. If you sincerely believe, Sister, that I have taken a patient's life, whether through negligence or whatever, you are welcome to take a complaint upstairs. My conscience is clear. I'm sure that Mrs Thwaites' daughter will be more than happy to postpone the funeral until a full post-mortem has been undertaken on her vacant, bedbound, septuagenarian mother.

Calmer now. Magnanimous in victory.

She had heart failure, Sandra. And then a stroke. Sometimes the soul just knows when it's time to let the body go. We can't stop that, we can only delay it.

Scene 8

The prison cell.

FRED: I mean, it was fine. She never said owt to anyone else. Everyone knew I was a very good doctor, I'd passed all my exams. It was good in a way. It showed me I had to be more aware of my surroundings. To be discreet, less cocky, to cover my tracks. I discovered there were rumours and gossip on the ward. I was nearly stopped in my life's work practically before it had begun. It all got a bit bloody hot is the truth of it, so when the opportunity to work as a registrar in paediatrics came up, I grabbed it with both hands. New ward, new patients. Young patients, none of the little beggars was close to death.

There was this one kid, though. Susie. Only four years old, the poor little mite, your heart went out to her. She was quadriplegic, she had cerebral palsy and severe epilepsy as well. The fit that got her admitted to hospital had given her more brain damage, she couldn't even see come the end. I was trying to tell her mother that the prognosis wasn't good, that while we could keep her alive with strong meds, there was no getting better; she'd never be well. It would only prolong her suffering. So when her mum said to me "Be kind to her", and gave her a kiss, and then went away to get a cup of tea, I knew what she meant. What she was asking of me. It confirmed to me in my mind that every aspect of my work was good and just and right. I could tell when a patient's time was due, and my judgement was sound.

Anyroad, I might have known that, but I knew my other colleagues were neither as certain, nor as blessed with my clarity of thought. After I was done in paediatrics, I switched to Obstetrics and Gynaecology. I got on well enough, I like kids and babies, always have done. But it wasn't a stimulating career move, by any means. I mean, what's the mystery? People have been birthing babies since the dawn of time, it doesn't call for any particular skill. The only thing that did catch my interest at the time was pethidine: I was struck by the serenity it brought the mothers in their moment of need. It cut right through the pain of childbirth, it took them to somewhere peaceful on the other side. I tried it myself, to alleviate my own boredom, as much as anything else. I stuck it out in obstetrics for six months, and then at last, my number came up – I saw an ad for a position as a probationary general practitioner at a busy group practice in Todmorden! Finally, four years after graduating, my dream had come true – I was a GP, free to practice the full range of medicine with my very own list of patients.

I tell you, after the tedium of obstetrics, I flourished in Todmorden. I was the driving force behind a new system for storing patient data,

33

and I undertook to dispose of some out-of-date medications in the practice's supply cabinet. And having removed the out-of-date medications, I was sure to order more with which to restock it. I put some aside for myself, of course. Some pethidine, which I'd got a taste for... and some morphine, should the need for it arise.

It was Wednesday, the week after my birthday. January 21st. I'd just turned 29. I went to see Elizabeth Pearce at her home, there was no-one else there. She wasn't well – she was frail, short of breath. The family had set up a bedroom on the ground floor, so she didn't have to be up and downstairs all the time. And I could see it, clear as day - what she had to look forward to. They said she'd been celebrating over Christmas, but how could she have been? Really? She... (*beat*) She reminded me of my mum come the end.

Scene 9

Vera Shipman's bedroom. Light and sound as before - the radio is now playing a selection of early 60s hits. Fred steps into the light with a cup of tea (mimed).

FRED: Here you go Mum, nice cup of tea, perk you right up.

It's a quarter to five. He won't be long now.

I know, Mum, it's the pain talking, I know that.

Forgive you? What on earth for?

For God's sake, it's not your fault. It's not your fault!

I wish I could stop it. I wish I could take all this away for you.

Some bloody son I turned out to be. No, Mum, I'll say my piece. All that money you spent, all that scrimping, and I still can't do owt for you! I can't FIX you, and it kills me, Mum! It kills me.

I'm sorry. I will. I will, I'll make you proud. And you'll see. You just hang on long enough, and I'll get my training, and I'll make you right as rain. I swear.

That'll be him now. I'll turn this rubbish off and go let him in. Soon feel better, eh?

Scene 10

The prison cell.

FRED: Everything I couldn't do for my Mum, I could do for Lizzie Pearce. All the suffering. Head it off at the pass. A whole family's pain, cut short in an instant. I wrote it up as a stroke, caused by blocked arteries. It was plausible enough. I sat with her, watching her relax as the morphine did its work. After a few minutes, she passed on, I packed my bags and left to go back to the surgery. And as I walked down the road, I felt again what I had first felt in Pontefract, that... elation, that pride. I had taken away pain and misery, and I had decided whether someone lived or died. I'd saved her family distress. In Pontefract, I was finding my way. I was learning what drugs worked best, and everyone I helped had been suffering so long already. No, this time I saw that grief coming, and I stopped it.

I had to do it again. I had to prove to myself I was right. I'd been back at Todmorden an hour or so, looking for a suitable candidate, when a call came through. He wasn't one of my patients – he belonged to Grieve – but I was on late duty, and it was my job to make house calls after hours. Lingard, his name was. Bob. He was only young, really, only 62, but he was very poorly. He had emphysema. And I knew that this was a test for me. I couldn't leave the man coughing

36

and spluttering, gobbing up phlegm all over himself. What sort of a life was that? Or his wife, his son, cleaning up after him? Grieve had made it an easier decision to take – he'd already told Lingard's boy that Bob didn't have long to go.

I hesitated. It was a mistake. I got there, I looked Bob over, I could see he was done for. Another one smoked his way to an early grave. I was talking to his wife, trying to find an excuse to come back in the next few days… and in that moment he died. He died, without my permission. It was my duty to say when he died, and he presumed to decide for me.

He catches himself, stops the tape, rewinds it to "I hesitated. It was a mistake."

…and in that moment, he died. I should have helped him the moment I saw him, and in not doing so, he went full of pain, coughing his filthy lungs up. I did my best to comfort his widow, but how much easier would have been for her if it'd been peaceful?

I had to fix it. I had to show death that I was its master, that there would be no more agonised passing on my watch. Then Lily Crossley's husband called. Poor Lily. Lung cancer, like my mum again. But it was metastatic, a tumour was growing on her shoulder. Bed-bound as she was, it was giving her so much pain. I was already giving her pethidine for it. She'd been getting agitated, struggling out of bed. It was time. I was impulsive, I can see that now; I'd never be that reckless again. Or not often, anyroad. I wasn't out of control, I knew I had to exercise some caution. I'd been present at two deaths in one day. It wouldn't do to be there for a third, people would ask questions. So I undertook an interesting experiment: instead of injecting the morphine intravenously, I injected it into her muscles.

The difference, you see, is in the speed of delivery. With Lizzie Pearce, I gave her the shot, and she died in front of me. It was as if the power of her life left her and entered me. But with Lily, it took far longer for the morphine to do its work; I was safely back at home with Prim by the time Lily's husband saw her pass. Who could possibly suspect the nice young man who'd given her her regular shot earlier that evening? Of course, as a responsible physician, I took possession of the pethidine she'd been prescribed. I'd use it still for the next year. But that day, a weight had fallen from my shoulders; I had an inkling, even then, that I'd soon not need it anymore.

I'd started blacking out at work. I was using more heavily, to stave off the next time I could feel that way again. I needed to be careful about how often I helped someone, I couldn't draw attention to myself. I couldn't risk a repeat of Pontefract. On the other hand, when you understand the gift you've got, how can you in good conscience neglect it? So I used the pethidine to tide me over, if you like, and it messes you up. It's fine as a temporary painkiller, but not for prolonged use. My veins collapsed; I was fainting, like I say – I concussed myself once. The old bill were sniffing around the surgery anyway, I'd been prescribing the stuff too much and they knew summat was afoot. I had to, to keep my supply coming in. Anyroad, in late September they worked out I was using it for myself, and I had to go to rehab for three months. I said it was because I didn't like my colleagues – Grieve, Dacre and the rest – but that wasn't it. Not all of it. I've worked with worse, that's for sure. I went through rehab and I came out clean, determined never to be in thrall to anything ever again.

I pleaded guilty to eight charges in the end, of obtaining and unlawfully possessing pethidine, and of forging prescriptions. I asked for another 74 offences to be taken into account. All about how I got the stuff. It was canny, you see – by being upfront, by being completely upfront, I got to keep my licence. I could still practise medicine, so I got a job in Durham, working in the Community Child Health Service.

It was a good job. Like I said, I like kids, but it was not my true calling. So after 18 months or so, I applied for, and got a job in a seven-doctor practice in Donneybrook, in Hyde. Hyde's an industrial town, used to have a colliery, textile factories, all that. Mostly, though, it's famous for three people: LS Lowry, the painter, Ian Brady and Myra Hindley. There's a lot of elderly folk in Hyde. It was a trying time. I had much work to do, but I simply could not gain access to the drugs I needed. One of the conditions of my freedom to practise medicine was that I wasn't allowed to carry controlled drugs in my medical kit. And without my morphine, I could not act, even if I could see that it was a person's time.

I had to gather my drugs opportunistically, scraping them together piecemeal. Like a tramp building a scruffy roll-up from discarded fag-ends picked up off the street. It was undignified. A patient who died of cancer might have a few ampoules of morphine lying around here and there that I could appropriate – if I could find them. I still did house visits, not like your so-called GPs nowadays, too high and mighty to put in the time with poor old dears too frail to make the journey into town. That was good, it afforded me the occasional windfall: a patient who needed a morphine injection and had the drugs at home. I could put her out of her pain, ease her on her way, and then take the excess for my next deserving case.

It wasn't good enough, though. I remember one woman, Alice Gorton. She was in a bad way. She had chronic psoriasis, which is a nasty, disfiguring skin disease.

Crossing to the bed, he picks up the three torn strips of sheet, rolls them up one by one like bandages and puts them on the table.

I saw her regularly to put fresh ointments and dressings on her skin, and I realised: it'll never get better for you, will it? Life, I mean. And I had a little morphine left over from a patient who'd died a week earlier, and I thought well, why not? I calculated that I had enough to see her off, but she held on, and slipped into a coma. It was bloody nerve-wracking - I'd given her the injection, and I went down to the front room to call her daughter and tell her to get over to the house. When she got there, I was just telling her there'd be no need for a post-mortem when we both heard a groan from the bedroom – she wasn't dead!

He takes a quick pause to calm down, regather his thoughts.

She wasn't dead. I'd made her life immeasurably worse, which was anathema to me. I'd failed her, and what's more, I'd failed myself – I was in considerable danger. What if she woke up? What if they took her to hospital? What if she died and they did a post-mortem and found she had morphine in her system? In the end, I persuaded her daughter to keep her in bed, and she passed away at home the next day. I put it down to a stroke, and she never did get a post-mortem. I was in the clear – for the moment.

Three months later, the same thing happened again. Jack Shelmerdine, he had chronic bronchitis and heart failure. I gave him some morphine, which I hoped would stop his already ropey breathing. But again, it wasn't enough, and he fell into a coma as well. His son wrote a letter of complaint to the Regional Health Authority, not about me, thank God, but still. I had to write a letter confirming I'd given morphine to a man with chronic bronchitis! Another patient whose gentle release I had botched. Two comas in three months. What a mess. What misery for the relatives. I resolved then and there, I would have to stop. I was making things worse.

Scene 11

Vera Shipman's bedroom. Fred enters, gesturing someone into the room.

FRED: He's here, Mum. Doctor Campbell's here at last. She's in a bad way, Doctor, it's been a hard day today.

What are you listening for, doctor? Are you listening for crepitations in the lungs?

Oh. Right. A pulse. Of course.

It's alright Mum, it'll make you feel better.

Don't talk daft, I'll still be here.

I'll come up when you're a bit less woozy. I love you, Mum.

Fred steps away from the bed shyly.

Thank you, Doctor.

Is there no chance at all, Doctor? Are you sure she'll never recover?

How can you know, though? She's so young, she's not 50 yet. People don't get cancer till they're old, surely? She's never smoked, won't allow it in the house, she...

He hardens, sceptical of the doctor's "expertise".

I'm not stupid. I came top of the class in my biology test today, 84%.

Is there really nowt you can do to make it easier? I hate seeing her like this.

I'd better be getting on. Got to walk Clive home from school. Thank you, Doctor, I'll see you out.

Scene 12

The prison cell. Fred picks up the rolled strips of sheet, ties the three ends together in a knot and begins pleating them into a rope.

FRED:　　　My time inactive wasn't wasted – I was rapidly establishing myself a well-deserved reputation as the best doctor in Hyde, and I was thinking about the ways I could do my work while avoiding detection. I found that I could use the excuse of taking a blood sample to explain away injection marks; and if I was visiting someone in sheltered accommodation, I could make use of the warden in establishing an alibi.

It's tricky, you see. You know you're doing the right thing, but you know just as well that other people might not see it like that. The relatives don't realise that you're sparing them pain, too. You're taking away their mum's or their dad's or their little girl's suffering, absolutely, and some of them might even understand that if their loved one's already in agony; but if you spot it in time, see that inevitable slope towards death, and you can stop it before it starts... well, you're also taking away their pain, the relatives' pain. You're saving them from the quiet horror of sitting downstairs or in the next room, feeling the seconds pass like hours, as you watch someone you love die by infinitely small degrees.

Or not watch them, as often as not, now I think about it. It's hard for folk to see what infirmity does to a body, and not feel a measure of revulsion. Or pity, which can be worse. It's why we stick them in nursing homes by the dozen, and leave them there to endure a managed decline at best. Can't face watching grandad go doolally and start wetting himself? Let someone else look after him, and return him to you a freshly washed corpse. Because that decline is terrible to see, we know what it means: it's the memento mori, the harbinger of what's to come. It's the irrefutable proof that your Mum may not be the God you thought she was as a small boy, and the promise of the frailty that awaits us all in our time.

So I had to be discreet. I always had to maintain a level of furtiveness, of deniability. It gave the whole business an air of grubbiness. I wasn't ashamed of what I was doing. I was simply aware that most people lacked my clarity of vision. At my surgery once, a patient of mine who worked as a home help mentioned that she'd discovered a couple of dead bodies over the years in the course of her work. I wondered if she were trying to tell me something; if she were reaching out to me as a kindred spirit. I asked her, did she find it gave her a buzz, finding a body? She said she found it very upsetting. I remember Mavis Pickup, her husband had just died of a heart attack – a real one. I decided she'd be best off joining him, and while I waited for the funeral director, I had the idea to bring my boy in to see the body – he was waiting for me in the car, you see. I don't know why, exactly; I think perhaps I hoped he'd want to follow in his old dad's footsteps one day, to become a doctor. He didn't want to, though, I think he was squeamish. I'm proud of the boy, but sometimes I think he's got too much of Prim in him if I'm honest.

I remember when that animal shot all them kids in Dunblane. I had a patient come to see me a day or so after, and the case came up. We weren't being morbid, everyone was talking about it. And I remember she was so angry that he'd killed himself. I said why, she said he should have been taken alive so society could punish him. So I said to her, I said, so you think he should be behind bars then? She said no, he should have been taken alive so that we could hang him! So I said you wanted him to survive, so that society, which means you and me, could kill him? And she said yes! And I said to her, I said well, duck, if you want to kill somebody to slake your own lust for justice, how different are you from him? Ooh, she left in a proper huff. A case of chronic stupidity, that one. Prognosis terminal.

Anyroad, after a few years, I felt I was sufficiently respected in Hyde that I could get away with carrying morphine in my medical kit again without anyone bringing up the pethidine unpleasantness. Turns out I needn't have worried: well, you don't ask after the contents of another doctor's kit, do you, and my patients wouldn't have understood what a controlled drugs ban meant even if they knew about it. And with my difficulties behind me, I then hit on a solution to getting a regular supply. Morphine's commonly prescribed for people in late stage cancer to help them with the pain. So I'd prescribe patients with a bit more than they'd need here and there; and in my capacity as a very good doctor renowned for going the extra mile, I'd call into the pharmacy to collect it for them, tell them how much to take, and keep the excess for my own purposes. In the end, I realised I could just prescribe it for folk, collect it for them, and they'd never even know they were supposed to be on it! I'd gather enough morphine, and I'd keep a weather eye out for someone who needed my tender mercies. Once a month. Maybe two or three if the need became too great, then I'd cool off for a few months. I knew I couldn't risk arousing suspicion, but then I'd have to feel that rush again. Something would get me right down, an argument with a nurse, or some bloody know-it-all would question my judgement, and I'd have to get back on top.

It's funny though: when I look back on it, relatives would just accept what I told them, by and large. Heart attack, stroke, old age. I'd tell them it was peaceful – which it was – and that their mum had just had a heart attack – which is anything but peaceful – and they'd just go along with it. Death, and my control of it, made me feel more alive, more alert, more myself than anything; but most folk, it'd just shut them down completely. It's the final taboo, isn't it? It's the thing we can't face up to, in others or in ourselves. Most of the time, I could tell the most outrageous whoppers, and they'd never question it. They wanted to believe their mum or dad had had an easy death, is the truth of it. That was the way of things: you don't question the doctor. Don't WANT to question the doctor! He knows better. As me mum always said, there's none so blind as them who will not see, and there's no end to what folk will not see when you're rich, or powerful, or a pillar of the community.

Take Jim. In '96, Jim came to me in terrible pain. He was a great help to me, was Jim King – for a while. The cancer unit at the local hospital diagnosed him with prostate cancer, and they had him on chemo. I got a letter from the oncologist instructing me to prescribe him morphine, and I was happy to oblige. Six weeks later, it turned out they'd loused up the diagnosis, and even though he was still in pain, he didn't have cancer, and they said he should start coming off the morphine. I simply delayed a bit on weaning him, is all.

He was such a good source of the stuff, I was helping all manner of other patients thanks to him. Then the oncologist got wind he'd been on morphine for nine months longer than he should have been, so I had to put a stop to it sharpish.

Scene 13

The Market St surgery, July 1997. Early morning, with the sounds of Hyde gearing up for its Saturday shop in the background.

FRED: Come on in Jim, sit yourself down.

I'll get right to the point: you've won the lottery. You don't have cancer – and what's more, you never did!

I'm not sure about all the ins and outs, but I believe it was a mix-up with the house surgeon at the cancer unit back in November.

Well, now. You might want to consult a lawyer. I've already consulted my own, and we're pretty sure I'm in the clear, but still. It's the right thing to do, and if they find any sort of wrongdoing on my part, I will face the consequences.

That's something you'll have to talk over with Deb.

Well, I have to say, you don't seem very pleased. You're a well man, Jim!

No, I don't see any need to keep you on the morphine. Coming off it will be unpleasant for a few days or so, I'm not going to lie, but then you'll be right as rain.

Methadone, you're thinking of. I can't see as how that would be appropriate in your circumstances. Cold turkey's the best way, believe me – there's a million folk out there, they shake one addiction just to form another.

I don't see as how I'm in any way responsible. It's a matter of willpower.

I didn't repossess your car. I didn't cost you your job.

You must do what you feel is right, Jim, but I will not prescribe you methadone. It's inappropriate.

You must find a spine if you can, go into rehab if you must, but you'll get no more drugs from me. Good day to you.

Scene 14

The prison cell.

FRED: How dare he question me. I knew what Jim was going through, I'd been there myself. If I was capable of coming out of it, then so was he. And if he wasn't, well, his lack of character was no concern of mine, was it? He started a medical negligence claim against me, for all the good it did him. I simply stuck to the immutable truth: I treated him appropriately for his medical condition at the time. I got my own back in the end, though: I bumped his dad off that Christmas Eve. How's that for a Christmas present.

Things went on as usual for a while; my urges would get stronger or weaker; I might get greedy, or encounter someone who said to me, said to my face that they'd had enough, and what was I to do, ignore that? I had a few firsts, now and then. In 1989, I helped Mary Hamer along in the surgery itself, and while she lay in the examination room, I saw three other patients. It was exhilarating, *thrilling*: taking her life, then tending to other people in the next room, all the while knowing she was lying there. At any point, it could turn out that one of them would need to go into the examination room. Another doctor might need to pop in, grab a swab or summat! I felt giddy with the knowledge of it, intoxicated on my own power.

I couldn't do it often, of course, only about five times as I recall, but oh, when I did…!

Every so often, I'd help too many at a time; four in a week, say, or three over a Christmas, and I'd hear mutterings at Donneybrook, and I'd have to stop for a while. Months at a stretch, I'd have to go. I started to hate them there, sticking their ignorant noses into my business. I ran that bloody place, I made all manner of innovations, but were they grateful? Were they hell as like. So in 1992, I took the plunge and set up my own surgery as a sole practitioner. The Surgery on Market Street opened on August 24th, 1992; it was my finest achievement, in many ways. I was free to work with who I wanted, employ staff I trusted, unimpeded by the judgement of my so-called peers. I took my patient list with me from Donneybrook; six weeks later, I had my next case in need of my special attentions.

It made getting hold of morphine substantially easier, working on my own. And finally, a medical advance resolved the issue more or less entirely. From the late 80s or so, a device called a syringe driver became the norm for issuing regular pain relief through subcutaneous injection. It was revolutionary: it enabled me to pick up 100mg ampoules, in tens, boxes of them at a time. My days of scrabbling to put together a single shot were long behind me, oh yes. I could collect 3,000 milligrams of the stuff without query, and at 30 milligrams per go, I had more of the stuff than I could get through.

My mastery of life and death was complete. I decided the fate of everyone who came my way. I'll admit that, sometimes, I was a pinch zealous. If someone defied me, or thought they knew better, or just proved themselves too much of a bloody nuisance, it was so very easy to put them out of my misery, if you follow me. Mostly, though, it was people who'd run out of life, but couldn't let go. Ravaged with cancer, with heart disease, with Alzheimers.

Scene 15

It feels at first like Vera Shipman's room – same lighting, same suburban sounds. Then a roaring car goes by, blaring a snippet of a '97 pop song.

Fred steps into the light, a doctor's bag in his hand (all mimed), every inch the concerned, kindly doctor.

FRED: Hello? Renee love?

Hello Renee, it's me. I said I'd pop by today.

Renee, love, it's me. It's Fred? Doctor Shipman? You remember me, don't you? I was here about a week back.

He checks her pulse.

It's all right, Renee.

You're in a bit of a way, aren't you, Renee love? Can you sit up for me, dear? I know it's hard.

Taking out a stethoscope, he listens to her lungs.

How's Anne? Has she had her baby yet? And your other one, Eileen? Is she still around, or did she go back down south?

Putting the stethoscope back, Fred takes a syringe out of his bag and fits it with a needle.

She was here a few weeks ago, do you not remember? Brought her boy, didn't she? That's nice.

Renee, love, it's me. It's Dr Shipman. There's nothing to be afraid of. I'm your doctor, I'm just going to take a quick blood sample. See if we can't find out what's making you so tired.

You're still smoking, I see. I've told you, you mustn't, it's not good for you, you know.

Fred takes an ampoule out of his bag, and jabs the needle into it, drawing the plunger back to fill the cylinder with fluid.

Now, I know you've been feeling scared and confused, Renee, and what with the cancer, you're feeling very flat. But this'll make everything a bit easier, all right?

No, there's nothing to worry about. You're lucky to have me, you know. There's lots of folk would kill to take your place on my list! Can you give me your hand, Renee love? Here we go, just a sharp scratch. That's it. All done now.

By this point, Fred is breathing heavily, taken by some obscure ecstasy. After a pause, as its grip on him lessens, he calls behind him:

Jim? Could you come up here? Quite quickly, I think she's slipping away.

Scene 16

The prison cell.

FRED: Once they were gone, my duty was to the living and not the dead. I'd orchestrate the funeral arrangements for the relatives, who were generally not in a fit state to think about such things. Obviously, I'd steer them towards cremation...

Market Street thrived. My patient list grew from 2,000 to 3,200 at its biggest, though that was just too many, I had to let some go. Sometimes, someone would get my back up. Patients. Their families. They'd doubt me. They had the nerve to question my judgement. Had a few hypochondriacs; people who insist there's summat wrong with them when they're the very picture of health, I could not abide them. I know where it comes from, of course. Psychologically. They're trying to control death. Trying to keep the inevitable at bay, to anticipate every problem. What it told me, in fact, was that they didn't trust me. They presumed to know my job better than I did. I couldn't have that, I'd not have someone stepping on my toes. No indeed, I would not let that pass. The one thing you could say for them, they never gave me any trouble come the end.

Come 1998, I was at the peak of my powers. It didn't matter, by that point, if you were sick yet. I could see, from your lifestyle, from your background, from your genetics, what would do for you. I was disposing of up to three people a month, almost one a week. People'd ask questions from time to time. I came close to being caught in flagrante once or twice, but I could talk my way out of anything. Then one day in early April, my old pal Alan Massey, from Massey's the funeral directors, paid the surgery an unexpected visit.

Scene 17

The Market St surgery, April '98. Late afternoon, the lights bright. The local school in Hyde is letting out for the day in the background.

FRED: Alan! This is a surprise. Come to try and get on my list, have you? Come in, come in.

Oh, right. Well, sit down and let's talk.

Rumours?

Chinese whispers, is that it?

Your Deborah's made a report to the coroner? Saying what, exactly?

I see.

Well, there's a perfectly rational explanation for it. We're a month out of winter, and deaths always go up over winter, you should know that more than anyone. Flu, the cold, nasty slips on ice. All the usual ailments and then some.

Just how long has Deborah had these concerns? She's never said owt to me.

Well, have no fear, Alan. It's all in the book, and anyone can have a look at my book. It's open for inspection by any of the authorities as want to see it.

No, the police haven't been to see me, no. How long back did they interview you?

Well, that's a good sign then, in't it? If there was owt to worry about, I'm sure they'd have been round already.

No, don't worry yourself. I'm grateful if I'm honest. I'm very glad you've come to me with this, as a friend and as a colleague. I'll put it all straight, don't you worry.

Alright, ta-raa then. Take care. Love to Deb!

Fred slumps, sweating, shaken to the core.

Scene 18

The prison cell.

FRED: Jesus, he put the wind up me. I stopped immediately. The stockpiling, the faked medical records, the... deaths, the lot. It didn't come to owt. The initial complaint. No-one could add it all up, I was too clever for them, but I couldn't handle the stress. I started thinking about all those bodies in the graveyards, the ones I hadn't been able to send to the crem. Morphine takes a hell of a long time to decay in a corpse, it lingers for years. What if they started digging them up? Every new death certificate had me panicking, whether I was responsible or not. Every time I picked up a prescription, I was expecting the approach, the polite cough, the "help with our inquiries". But then the stress made the need more urgent, I'd have to get back up on top, so I'd give in and I'd see another old dear over the threshold, and that drove up the pressure even more. It was intolerable.

I couldn't cope anymore; the pressure, the risk, the hunger, the loathing, I couldn't bear it. I had to bring a stop to it. I'd despaired of them ever catching me. I'm in here, aye, but it's nowt to do with them, no-one outwitted me. You think I stopped because some bright spark put two and two together? Oh, no. No, I got caught because I decided it was time.

I came up with the idea to forge a will. Local councillor, had two houses. Kathleen Grundy her name was. At the surgery one day, I tricked her into signing a form that was actually a blank will, asked a couple of waiting patients to sign as witnesses, and then I typed it up as a new will and sent it to a local firm of solicitors. In it, she left everything to me, "to reward him for all the care he has given to me and the people of Hyde." Quite right, too.

The way I saw it, either her daughter – who was also her solicitor – would be fooled, I'd be quids in, and I could leave Hyde, leave Prim and the kids, leave medicine and all the rest of it behind, go and live out my days on some beach somewhere; or she'd see through it, and this need, this monstrous, gnawing need would finally be over.

I did for Grundy on June 24th; I wrote to the solicitors I'd sent the forged will to, but nowt happened. By the start of July, I'd just about resigned myself to never getting out of the cycle, I got hold of another 100mg of morphine, when finally! News broke that the police were investigating the will in late August. I continued to work at Market Street of course, I had obligations to my patients; but I was done. I'd finally drawn enough attention to myself for them to stop me. They arrested me on September 7th, 1998. I tried to brazen it out, but I'd trapped myself too well. I've been in custody ever since.

The press were predictably disgusting. Doctor Death, they called me. I was charged with fifteen murders – one of the redtops said I was responsible for fifteen hundred! As far as I can tell, they simply estimated how many death certificates I'd issued during my whole career and then doubled it for good measure. Bloody ghouls. Baying for my blood. I remember a few years back, I'd not been inside long, it was in the papers that Brady that kiddie-murdering little prick had gone on hunger strike; said he wanted to die. Anyroad, the Sport ran a headline, it said summat like "Ian Brady Wants To Starve Himself To Death, So Send Him A Pork Pie!" People say they want justice, but they don't. Not really. What they want is power. They want to play God. They've no concept of what that means. What it takes. I had that power, I had the brilliance to wield it. The local rag did a survey of my patients when I went down for the fifteen, and seven out of ten of them would have me back if I were released tomorrow. That's how good I was, how respected I was in the community.

Since they sent me down, they've added another 200 or so to the tally of "victims", as they put it. They think I did more, but they don't know, for all the good their inquiry did them. I haven't read the report, I'm not going to. I wouldn't help them with it, even when they went right back to Todmorden. I never said a word. As for the courts, they've no control over me now. Imbeciles. The minute they put me in here for life, they threw away all their leverage. They can't bully or cajole anything out of me. I could sit here for 40 years if I wanted, like Brady. The power's all mine, like it always has been. I still get respect in here. They call me doctor. They come to me for advice - minor ailments, that sort of thing. Imagine what I could do for them if I had my drugs.

Prim spoke to them. That stung. Shouldn't be surprised, I suppose – she was never strong, not like me. She didn't have owt to be afraid of, but she was always like that. Weak. Can't blame her, really, but still. I have to think of her, now, and the kids. I have to do what's best for them.

It's no life in here. It's not like I can't take it - I said to a friend a few months back, I said if I could cope with being a junior houseman at Pontefract General, then prison life is certainly no worse. No, I don't want to live out my days being associated with murderous scum like West and Sutcliffe. Christie. I'm not like them, all sweaty id and uncontrollable lust. We're not even the same species, how dare anyone lump me in with animals like them. I treated people appropriately for their medical condition at the time. If I say your time is coming, and you say I'm talking nonsense, what else am I to do? I'll not have my judgement questioned. Your time is your time, that's for me to decide. I am a very good doctor. I have passed all my exams. I'll decide when you'll die. Me. I've had the mastery of life and death for thirty years. And I tell you this, I would kill every last one of my patients when I see fit, because they belong to me!

Fred stops the recorder, ejects the tape and destroys it.

Then he takes his specs off, puts them in his top pocket, picks up the rope and begins to tie a crude noose.

They think, because they've locked me up, that they control me now. But no-one controls me. No man will ever bid me. They think they've stopped me killing, well they've got another think coming. I will choose the time of my passing, and the manner of it. I've always said "I don't believe in keeping 'em going." I stand by that.

Fred stands directly centre stage, spot-lit, the completed noose in his hand, and freezes as the lights fade, leaving the name projections as the only stage illumination, and the closing voice-over plays.

NEWSREADER: (*V/O*) ...That was Harriet Cass reporting, the time is now ten past eight. The Home Secretary, David Blunkett, is facing criticism for remarks made yesterday in response to serial killer Harold Shipman's suicide. Shipman, who was convicted of murdering 15 people and found responsible for killing 200 more over a period of

26 years, was found hanged in his cell at Wakefield Prison on Tuesday morning.

At an informal lunch for London-based regional journalists, Blunkett is reported to have said: "You wake up and you receive a phone call – Shipman's topped himself. You have just got to think for a minute: is it too early to open a bottle? And then you discover that everybody's very upset that he's done it."

He then added that he had to be very careful about what he said in his job...

The projection of the names fades out.

A NOTE ON THE VICTIMS

Dr Harold Shipman was convicted of fifteen murders and, at the conclusion of the Smith Inquiry, was ultimately found responsible for having killed 218 people over 26 years. He is also suspected of having killed up to 85 more people, particularly early on in his career, but Dame Janet Smith concluded that it was impossible to rule on those deaths with sufficient certainty.

In writing this play, I made the choice to characterise four specific cases from those suspected deaths as murders for the sake of the story. All of them are mentioned by name in the text, so their absence from the projection on the wall would appear to the audience to be a glaring omission.

As a result, the following list consists of 222 names, not 218; these are the names that should be projected onto the back wall during performance.

* - denotes a murder where a conviction was secured

1972
Thomas Cullumbine (54)

Elizabeth Thwaites (74) (suspected)

John Brewster (84)

James Rhodes (71)

Susie Garfitt (4) (suspected)

1975
Lily Crossley (73) (suspected)

Elizabeth Pearce (84) (suspected)

Eva Lyons (70)

1978

Sarah Hannah Marsland (86)

Mary Ellen Jordan (73)

Harold Bramwell (73)

Annie Campbell (88)

1979

Alice Maude Gorton (76)

Jack Leslie Shelmerdine (77)

1981

May Slater (84)

Elizabeth Ashworth (81)

1983

Percy Ward (90)

Moira Ashton Fox (77)

1984

Dorothy Tucker (51)

Gladys Roberts (78)

Joseph Bardsley (83)

Winifred Arrowsmith (70)

Mary Winterbottom (76)

Ada Ashworth (87)

Joseph Vincent Everall (80)

Edith Webberley (76)

Eileen Theresa Cox (72)

1985

Peter Lewis (41)

May Brookes (74)

Ellen Higson (84)

Margret Ann Conway (69)

Kathleen McDonald (73)

Mildred Robinson (84)

Thomas Moult (70)

Frances Elizabeth Turner (85)

Selina Mackenzie (77)

Vera Bramwell (79)

Fred Kellett (79)

1986

Deborah Middleton (81)

Dorothy Fletcher (74)

Thomas Fowden (81)

Mona Ashton White (63)

Mary Tomlin (73)

Beatrice Toft (59)

Lily Broadbent (75)

James Wood (82)

1987

Frank Halliday (76)

Albert Cheetham (85)

Alice Thomas (83)

Jane Frances Rostron (78)

Nancy Anne Brassington (71)

Margaret Townsend (80)

Nellie Bardsley (69)

Elizabeth Ann Rogers (74)

1988
Elizabeth Fletcher (90)

Alice Mary Jones (83)

Dorothea Hill Renwick (90)

Ann Cooper (93)

Jane Jones (83)

Lavinia Robinson (84)

Rose Ann Adshead (80)

Alice Prestwich (69)

Walter Tingle (85)

Harry Stafford (87)

Ethel Bennett (80)

1989
Wilfred Chappell (80)

Mary Emma Hamer (81)

Beatrice Helen Clee (78)

Josephine Hall (69)

Hilda Fitton (75)

Marion Carradice (80)

Elsie Harrop (82)

Elizabeth Mary Burke (82)

Sarah Jane Williamson (82)

John Charlton (81)

George Edgar Vizor (67)

Joseph Frank Wilcockson (85)

1990
Dorothy Rowarth (56)

Mary Rose Dudley (69)

1992
Monica Rene Sparkes (72)

1993
Olive Heginbotham (86)

Hilda Mary Couzens (92)

Amy Whitehead (82)

Mary Emma Andrew (86)

Sarah Ashworth (74)

Fanny Nichols (84)

Marjorie Parker (74)

Nellie Mullen (77)

Edna May Llewellyn (68)

Emily Morgan (84)

Violet May Bird (60)

Jose Kathleen Diana Richards (74)

Edith Calverley (77)

Joseph Leigh (78)

Eileen Robinson (54)

Charles Edward Brocklehurst (90)

1994

Joan Milray Harding (82)

Christine Hancock (53)

Elsie Platt (73)

Mary Alice Smith (84)

Ronnie Devenport (57)

Cicely Sharples (87)

Alice Christine Kitchen (70)

Maria Thornton (78)

Henrietta Walker (87)

Elizabeth Ellen Mellor (75)

John Bennett Molesdale (81)

1995

Alice Kennedy (88)

Lucy Virgin (70)

Joseph Shaw (88)

Maria West (81) *

Netta Ashcroft (71)

Lily Bardsley (88)

Marie Antoinette Fernley (53)

John Crompton (82)

Frank Crompton (86)

Vera Brocklehurst (70)

Angela Philomena Tierney (71)

Edith Scott (85)

Clara Hackney (84)

Renata Eldtraude Overton (47)

Kate Maud Sellors (75)

Clifford Barnes Heapey (85)

Bertha Moss (68)

Brenda Ashworth (63)

Ernest Rudol (82)

Ada Matley Hilton (88)

Irene Aitken (65)

Arthur Henderson Stopford (82)

Geoffrey Bogle (72)

Dora Elizabeth Ashton (87)

Muriel Margaret Ward (87)

Edith Brock (74)

Charles Henry Barlow (88)

Konrad Peter Ovcar-Robinson (43)

Elizabeth Teresa Sigley (67)

Kenneth Wharmby Woodhead (75)

1996

Hilda Mary Hibbert (81)

Erla Copeland (79)

Jane Elizabeth Shelmerdine (80)

John Sheard Greenhalgh (88)

Minnie Doris Irene Galpin (71)

Marjorie Hope Waller (79)

John Stone (77)

Elsie Godfrey (85)

Edith Brady (72)

Valerie Cuthbert (54)

Lilian Cullen (77)

Renee Lacey (63)

Leah Fogg (82)

Gladys Saunders (82)

Nellie Bennett (86)

Margaret Mary Vickers (81)

Tom Balfour Russell (77)

Irene Turner (67) *

Carrie Leigh (81)

Marion Elizabeth Higham (84)

Elsie Hannible (85)

Elsie Barker (84)

Sidney Arthur Smith (76)

Dorothy Mary Andrew (85)

Anne Lilian Ralphs (75)

Millicent Garside (76)

Irene Heathcote (76)

Samuel Mills (89)

Thomas Cheetham (78)

Kenneth Ernest Smith (73)

1997
Eileen Daphne Crompton (75)

David Alan Harrison (47)

Elsie Lorna Dean (69)

Irene Brooder (76)

Charlotte Bennison (89)

Charles Henry Killan (90)

Betty Royston (70)

Joyce Woodhead (74)

Lizzie Adams (77) *

Rose Garlick (76)

May Lowe (84)

Mary Coutts (80)

Elsie Cheetham (76)

Jean Lilley (58) *

Lena Nora Slater (68)

Ethel May Kellett (74)

Doris Earls (79)

Ivy Lomas (63) *

Vera Whittingslow (69)

Maureen Lammonier Jackson (51)

Muriel Grimshaw (76) *

John Louden Livesey (69)

Lily Newby Taylor (86)

Dorothy Doretta Hopkins (72)

Nancy Jackson (81)

Mavis Mary Pickup (79)

Bessie Swann (79)

Enid Otter (77)

Florence Lewis (79)

Mary Walls (78)

Elizabeth Mary Baddeley (83)

Marie Quinn (67) *

Elizabeth Battersby (70)

Laura Kathleen Wagstaff (81) *

Bianka Pomfret (49) *

Alice Black (73)

James Joseph King (83)

1998

Mabel Shawcross (79)

Norah Nuttall (64) *

Cissie Davies (73)

Pamela Marguerite Hillier (68) *

Laura Frances Linn (83)

Irene Berry (74)

Maureen Alice Ward (57) *

Joan Edwina Dean (75)

Harold Eddleston (77)

Margaret Anne Waldron (65)

Irene Chapman (74)

Dorothy Long (84)

Lily Higgins (83)

Ada Warburton (77)

Martha Marley (88)

Winifred Mellor (73) *

Joan May Melia (73) *

Kathleen Grundy (81) *